# Where the Poems Grew

Brandy Harris

Copyright © 2026 Brandy Harris

All rights reserved.

ISBN: 979-8-234-01873-1

# DEDICATION

For the hopeless romantics,

the lovers

and all who know love.

# CONTENTS

# ACKNOWLEDGMENTS

Poetry was my first love. I have been writing since I was a little girl, and as I grew, poetry grew with me. It became a place where emotions, questions, and quiet moments could live on the page.

Sharing these words with you brings me both joy and a little nervousness, because this book holds pieces of my heart. Within these pages are some of my delicate poems, along with reflections that grew from experiences over time.

My hope is that as you read, you find something that resonates with you and something that brings comfort, healing, or understanding, just as poetry has done for me. More than anything, I hope these words remind you to believe in yourself and to keep chasing the dreams placed in your heart.

I am deeply grateful to everyone who has supported me on this journey of writing and healing. To my family and friends, thank you for your patience, encouragement and for listening when I needed to be heard.

# PART I – THE FIRST LIGHT

## Traditions

Traditions taught me:
Fall in love, get married, then have children
In that order.

Expectations told me:
Love must be all-consuming,
Constantly growing.

But I've learned
Sometimes love is complicated.

Sometimes I don't text back
When I have nothing to say.
Sometimes I wait to text back
To seem busy.
Sometimes I get the number
Then take days.

Sometimes falling on my face in love
Leaves bruises that everyone notices.

If I love him, sometimes it is just for a season.

If you make me smile and laugh,
I think I love you.
Then a few days later,
I'll contemplate if I ever did,
Or why I did.

Soulmates come from all directions.
They promise to love me,
Grow old with me,
Hold on to me.

But then the rain falls
And washes them away.

My mama taught me:
Love needs time to grow and expand.
Lonely seasons are necessary.
Marriage is not for everyone.

My daddy taught me:
Love can be found in every encounter.
There is something to take from it all.

Just because I leave teary-eyed at night,
Does not mean I will not have dry eyes by morning.

Social media teaches
Isolation and trusting no one.

Still, I am learning,
That life does not always follow traditions.

**Fantasies**

All my life I have chased around fantasies,
fantasies of the men I have dated
when we never really went on dates.

Fantasies that they would come save me
from this balcony,
Rescue me from myself.

They never showed up for me
I was always left wondering what it was
about myself, that was not good enough.

I did not have long hair like Rapunzel,
did not sleep well like Sleeping Beauty,
could not walk in heels to save my life,
I was no Cinderella.

I would never kiss a frog like Tiana,
loved too many beasts that never turned into gentleman,
unlike Belle.
The only thing I gained from loving them,
was the courage to love myself more.
The only thing left from the hurt,
was the strength to never feel it again.

One day I will find a love worth sacrificing for,
a love that will change my view on fantasies.

## Fall Season

This season called Fall
resembles my life every year,
old habits falling to the ground,
to make room for new things to appear.

## Fragile as Glass Coffee Cups

Today he almost gave up on us,
and I cried tears big enough
to fill glass coffee cups.

He's my spirit mate.
The last thing I would ever want
is to hurt him.

He doesn't deserve
the broken pieces of a woman.
He should never have to play clean-up crew
for the shattered glass of my heart.

He brings joy with him.
God knew I would need his smile
on the difficult days
his patience,
his gentle, steady spirit.

I never meant
to drag him through
my circus of emotions,
never meant to make him
walk tightropes
I hadn't learned to balance on myself.

I wanted to love him
in a healthy way.

But somewhere along the road
old wounds started speaking
louder than my intentions.
Fear dressed itself up as defense.
Silence turned into distance.

And today,
when he almost walked away,

I saw clearly,
that I could lose him.

## Wrapped in Conditions

Another man who only wanted
access to parts of me,
but never the depth of me.

He offered lavish trips,
all shine and sparkle,
while I quietly paid for most of it,
draining myself
financially
and emotionally.

He loved to speak about my appearance,
but could never communicate
about anything that mattered.

I was left feeling small
because I craved touch,
yet secretly
I craved a heart.

Every day I watched the shift.
The good morning texts
came later.

He stopped asking questions.
Stopped caring how my day had been.

In the beginning
he was everywhere,
inserting himself into my world,
convincing me
he would grow,
he would change,
eventually.

The chemistry was strong enough
that I tolerated what I shouldn't have

just to lie beside a man
who never called me beautiful,
never told me I was exceptional,
never invested in me,
only in the moment.

They play the role so well at first,
making promises that sound sweet
but mean nothing.

Then they change
as quickly as seasons do.

So tell me,

Why does your affection
shift with the weather?

Why was I never enough
to take seriously?

The trips would have been nice,
but it came wrapped in conditions.

I would have been your secret,
your convenience,
never your woman,
never your wife.

Maybe a friend.

But did you ever truly care?

**Inspired Love**

You have been the inspiration of love lately.
Every poem I craft carries a thought of you.
Every unhealed emotion begins to fade.

If you would do me the honor of knowing me,
of seeing me,
of sharing a smile,
I'd hold the thought of your face
in my mind out of the blue.

I don't want to downplay the way I feel.
I want you to know
that eventually I want more.
Because I believe it could be real.
Because I believe that with you
every lost moment,
would finally make sense.
Every past second would feel worthwhile.

Panic, baby.

Doesn't it hurt
to love someone and not be able to touch them,
not be able to feel them?

Doesn't it hurt
to not express that love,
to not care for them
when all you want
is to love them the way you believe they deserve?

You're panicking, aren't you?

Now you know how I felt.

When I cared for you,
it was constant rainy days,
hoping for an ounce of sunshine.

You showed me that some men
only care about what's inside,
and I'm not talking about the soul.

I'm talking about the part of me
that births children,
that creates generations,
that is so powerful
it can bring a man to his knees,
make him shed false tears,
make him chase youth,
make him promise forever,
make him lose himself.

Yet you treated it
like it was just
meant for selfish encounters.

I thought it was reciprocated love
when you just needed an escape.

You never cared about my view on things.
You never wanted to know what hurt me before
because somewhere deep down
you knew you would become part of that story.

So, no.
I don't miss you anymore.

I don't think of you gently.
Your face has changed in my mind.
Your sweetness no longer exists there.

You are not going with me into the future.
You will stay exactly where I left you
in the past,
where lessons live,
but love does not return.

Heartbreak changes you.
One day you are in love with who you are,
Because you think someone else loves you.

Then the next day you are falling back into old thinking,
Trying to remember what there is to love
about yourself because someone else
is not loving you.
Especially when you want them to,
Especially when it becomes difficult to.

There is purpose in the waiting,
for every closed road
leaves time to wonder.
No rush in having babies,
although every small smile
seems tempting.

**Sunrise Over Mountains**

The vast darkness
was swallowed
by purple, pink, and blue.

Colors so honest
I could only hope
to find beauty like that
within myself.

That hopeful morning
felt different.
Promising.
Powerful.

Once I hiked to the top,
I found a rock
that felt like home.

If God took me right then,
I would have gone gladly.

Where skies meet clouds.
Where stars make way for sunsets.
Where sunshine swears
fresh starts into existence.

New heights
mean new blessings.

Joy and truth do not hide here.

Browns.
Grays.
Greens.
Reds.

All hues of nature

holding infinite calm
and happiness.

Sunrise over mountains.

## A Million Light Years

We argued for hours
about my feelings,
the ones I tried so hard to express.

I got choked up just telling him,
scarred too much to even begin
to say I have had feelings for him
since college days.

We have always cared for each other,
our friendship far deeper than
the attraction we once shared.

He was a million light years
past loving me.
He said he did not want a relationship
because of the arguing it brings,
because carrying past pain
was too heavy.

I told him he would never get me
unless he meditated,
he said he would get it together one day.

I told him I do not usually
get tossed to the curb.

We are not together,
yet we argued for hours.

He is not my man,
and most likely
he will never be.

## The Perfect Love from a Narcissist

First things first
it was never perfect.
But that's how they get you,
rewind and retwist you,
make you think they fit you.

You provide the blueprint;
they study it as if they are masters,
use the tools of vulnerability
to get to you faster.

Truth is they would make great actors.
Pretend to care about
all the same things you are after.

Invested in your future,
only to use you.
Treat you like royalty in the beginning,
then they abuse you.

It will go from forehead kisses
to questioning if you matter,
and they will watch
while your heart shatters.

Do not tell them you are hurting,
it will only add fuel.
They will let you burn alive in agony,
and never believed they were cruel.

## Game Play

Y'all men really think y'all playing someone.

When I text, you pick up.
You show up.
You are right here next to me,
doing whatever I want,
and still, does it matter
if you do not say you love me?

Sometimes love hurts.
Actually, it always does.
And maybe I want you to hurt me
in ways that feel good to me.

I like the kind of man
that is all mine.
Makes me cherish it,
makes me feel like I can't replace it
even though I know I could.

Do not get it twisted.
It is all part of the game.
I know you love me.
Otherwise, you wouldn't waste your time on me.
I call, and you come.
So tell me, how's that not love?

You don't like saying it? I get it.
But it's how you are viewing it
that's ruining it.
Don't deny it when I ask.
You even got mad
that you had to say it.

So much anger there.
I've always known you were damaged,
but I will never know how deep.

So if you think it is best
to keep it that way,
I have said what I needed to say.
I have given you a piece of my healing spirit.

I gave you a refresher,
so go be great.

**Enduring**

Enduring looks like waking up every day
already too late,
dragging yourself out of bed
for a job you cannot stand
one that leaves you overworked,
underpaid,
and unseen.

The people who've "figured it out"
look at me like I should have too,
as if I missed some hidden door
they happened to find.

I'm tired of caring for everyone else's problems
while mine sit untouched.

Enduring feels like the heavy days,
the sad and questioning days
when the purpose of my existence
feels blurred at the edges.

Why do I work so hard
only to struggle?
Why must anxiety and depression
cling to me like a shadow?

If I cry or break down,
I am "too much,"
"too broken,"
better suited for giving advice
than needing it.

I breathe through the dark thoughts
the ones that whisper
that I do not deserve ease,
that giving up would be simpler,
that disappointment would end.

But still,
I breathe.

Even when it feels like no one sees me.
Even when I am convinced
they only miss versions of me
I have already outgrown.

I endure,
even when it hurts
and there is greatness in that.

**Access Denied**

Loving you came with a price tag.

Spending money on material things
when what I wanted from you
could not be bought.

My love came from a place of realness.
I gave you a sweet taste of my heart.
I sheltered your ego
as we came crashing down.

I built fences around reality
just to keep you in.
But you found your way out the back,
down the street,
across the nation.

It was inevitable
that you would leave.

All the locks and bolts I placed
on that home
I thought we were building together,
you slipped past them.
You found your way out
without even knowing the floor plan.

Truth is,
you were trespassing.
That place was never meant for you.

You fantasized about a life with me
made of jewelry, paparazzi, and bright lights.
You knew I was bigger
than you could ever be.

So instead,

you tried to humble me.
Tried to keep me small.
Keep me close enough
to benefit from the joy I carry,
the blessings I receive,
the light you thought you could leech from.

You tried to make me
one of your options.

But life would not let you tie me down.
Wouldn't let you anchor me
to a life beneath my calling.

You were never worthy
of a child with me.
Never worthy
of the title of my man.

And I'm grateful
I never told you I loved you.

Because I can only imagine
how you would have fed on
every vulnerable moment.

**All That**

If I did all that
Loved you and all that,
gave you all that,
treated you like you was *all that* -

then in fact,
I gave it all I could.

No should've, could've, would.
Real love – I understood.

I sought familiarity in your soul,
made stories with you that remain untold.

We shared a big secret we could not tell.
You always told me, *don't catch feelings*
although I always knew you well.

I never believed in ceilings,
there was always something beyond.
I gave up trying to read your mind.

You would tell me if I killed the mood.
You wanted my love on a platter,
just like your food.

**Fallen Stars**

Miscommunication creates distance,
all because of fear.
Too afraid to confront what is missing
instead we no longer share.

The common beliefs that kept us connected,
are now the same reasons we stay away.
False feelings of jealousy kept us projecting,
now the distance is growing bigger every day.

I miss our laughs and jokes,
miss realizing how beautiful a person you are.
I will never forget the many nights we stayed up
full of hope,
now you resemble much of fallen stars.
Too far out of grasp, I can only wish to know you again.
Only God knew my heart in this,
only God knew the end.

## To be Wanted

He asked, "Didn't you want this?"
Yes.

But who knew I would feel
as low to the ground afterwards
when he would pick that phone up
and go on about his life,
while I am panicking inside.

## The Truth About Us

I still think you are amazing
but it is just the way you made me feel
like an outsider that threw me off

It's the way I gave my all
and you gave me three boxes

It's the way I would have done anything
that made me realize I needed limits

So, like the beautiful skies I see
I'm blue but still bright
and I'll bounce back from this
like I have done everything else

And when I am on that operating table
I will come out a stronger woman than before

And I know that the love I had for you
was real but never reciprocated
and your love became too hard to find

Eventually the fantasy did not meet the reality

I was lying to my friends about you
but the truth is
nothing was true

## All Family Ain't Good Family

All family ain't good family
words my daddy used to say.
All family don't love you right;
some you have to keep away.

Some live for social media,
pretending their lives are grand.
But behind that glowing phone screen,
life dealt them a different hand.

Some claim they love you deeply,
down to their very bones.
But when the day comes that you transition,
they're selling everything in your home.

Some family only call you
when tragedy strikes.
They inspire these poems
Daddy told me their souls weren't right.

So, cry me a river,
or at least pretend to let tears flood,
'cause all family ain't good family,
even if they share your same blood.

## Ten Years, One Night

He would never know
that I cried.

While he was in the shower,
as he was looking for his clothes,
I was sniffling my nose.
He will not know I cried.

Great conversations mean nothing these days,
when I can talk to anyone.
Loving something means nothing,
when I have been taught to love everyone.

The truth will always be painful,
that I gave him my all,
it was never what he wanted.

He would always look for true forms of love in a different girl.
Yet keep me around for confidence.
Until he found someone he wanted to sacrifice for.

The most painful part,
I will never be his,
Despite the ten plus years of knowing him.

First night he treated me like an attractive woman,
the second night he treated me strictly like a friend.
I hated dating because of him.

## Kansas City

My city is a made-up dream,
Everyday my people are dying over made up things.

Full of black men
full of black kings,
they try to take them from us
because they are everything.

But we love them steadily,
Hold tight to them every night,
Kiss their lips before telling them,
do not go down without a fight.

# PART II – THE PRAYERS THAT SHAPED ME

## A Prayer for Self

Praying for me this time,
praying that I do not let anyone break me.

From this day forward, I'm praying for the strength
to let go of things that do not serve me,
even when I'm desperately trying to hold on.

I pray for peace with my body,
because it has taken its toll on me for too long.
I pray for brighter days,
full of prosperity and wisdom.

I pray for a love that doesn't leave me wondering,
a love I do not have to question,
a love that feels right
and on time.

I pray to succeed in my career,
to follow the path, I am meant to walk,
to use my gifts to make a difference.
God, I do not have all the answers,
but I know my purpose here can challenge me.

Sometimes I get caught up in the world,
but bring me back to me, God,
which ultimately brings me back to You.

I know I am here for bigger reasons
than to worry if someone loves me or not.
I'm here to spark change in the world,
to use my gifts,
to inspire,
and to be inspired by the people I meet along the way.

God, I pray for easier days.
I pray away the insecurities that form
when I start thinking too much.

An idle mind is the devil's playground.

I pray for a stronger mind,
to see past what is not right for me,
to know when the signs come from you, God.
I pray for proper discernment.

And so, it is.
And so, it will be.

## Psalm 23

The Lord is enough,
All I could ever need in this lifetime.
They way He gave His life so that mine
would be tolerable.
I am grateful.
Green pastures, make sure they are stocked with
my favorite flowers.
Lead me beside still waters, Lord
So, I may pray and give my worries to You.
All that I am and will become
Belongs to You.
I will always choose the righteous path.
Every good deed and blessing will be done
In your name.
Sometimes, I fear the things in this life, Lord.
Days can be dark and shallow.
But when I call out your name,
Those demons run,
afraid of your grace and power.
Omnipotent. Omnipresent.
With tools to keep me protected.
When they try to go low,
Because of your sacrificial love, I remain high.
You seat me at tables where those who
prey on my downfall
Have front row tickets
to watch me enjoy this feast
and fruitful life,
You have designed for me.
The blessings come heavy and in abundance.
Surely goodness along with mercy
Shall follow me all the days of my life
And I shall dwell in the house of the Lord forever.

**Prayer to Love**

My prayer is that I can love you the way
you deserve to be loved
That as God loved you,
I can aim for the same.

That through the trials and tribulations,
we will hold on to the best parts,
comfort each other through the bad parts,
and always remember that God was the one
who brought us together.

I never want to forget the beginning,
never want to look forward to an end
how we intuitively knew
we would share a connection from above.

The first time you wrote me, I was intrigued.
I loved that you loved God out loud,
with your actions and your words.

You seemed to understand me.
Held me accountable,
made me see things through the eyes
of the Holy Spirit.

We fellowshipped together,
recited Bible verses like our lives depended on it.
Talked of fleshy desires, hoping to combat them.
Believed that everything happened for a reason,
that God was with us in every season.

I grew stronger in faith with you.

Each day, you revealed that God was our fortress,
that we had nothing to fear.

Oh, how I pray to treat you right,

to not play with your feelings.

Yesterday I asked for clarity,
today, God is telling me:
you are a man of your word.
His soldier in the Holy Spirit
a man so deeply rooted in faith
that he would let go of anyone or anything
that would steer him away.

Just like me, you have come to the same conclusion.
We have traveled similar paths.

God, I will care for your child
do right by the man you sent into my life.
I trust him to lead,
trust his opinions,
trust his choices and decisions,
knowing he spoke to you before making them.

**Warm Embrace**

The comfort I found in Your warm embrace
the joy I could never forget
when Your love surrounded me.

The best and greatest love I had ever known
lives within the depths of You.

They talk of this God
known to be the one true God.

God is the one who resonates in my soul.
Just call this my Bible,
I've written love letters
straight to God.

God feels like beautiful beginnings
that never end.

God feels kind of like hope,
and love, and courage,
and all things good.

God feels better than evil,
it's hard even getting the words out sometimes.

I feel God's love as unconditional,
forever in my heart and spirit.

God's love never leaves.

So, I want to be like God.
I was made in His image.
My sins are forgiven.

**Spiritual Warfare**

God gave me the gifts
the favor and the love to get through it.

The enemy rode my coattail,
tried to get VIP access to my soul.

But I know the Word of God.
My anointing is my armor.

Despite the obstacles, I make it through,
surviving all that is to come.

Because this life I live,
had a purpose before I even got here.
I had meaning before I ever knew it.

There is a train coming
to carry me toward God's promises.

I used to miss it all the time.
Now I wait at the station,
checking the schedule,
making sure I don't miss it again.

Although the train will not come for a while,
I'll wait patiently.

**A Prayer to My Husband**

To the man who picked flowers
to put in my hair,

to the man who does not let me open doors,

to the one who asked for God's permission
to be with me,

to the one who called me Queen
and treated me like royalty,

to the man I never had to beg
to choose me

I love you.

I love waking up next to you,
feeling soft, easy days
sprinkled with everyday life.

Your cup was full before I met you,
yet you made room for me.
Now both our cups overflow.

Grace was evident in your life,
and your love for God inspired many,
including myself.

You always remind me
who I am in this world.

**Prayers to My Husband II**

Are you the one I will spend my life with?
Will you take me seriously forever?
Consider me your Queen
until eternity.

Will I find love
at the foot of our beds,
joy while opening the curtains each morning?

I will eat your breakfast in bed
while we share dinner with the kids
from a meal I cooked.
You'll make sure I never feel overworked
or overlooked.

You bring me smiles in the evenings,
sweet kisses above the covers.
I have never crossed that threshold with you,
but my heart already knows the wonder.

You hold my hand through tough times.
You are my peace in all the chaos.

You make me smile
the biggest, the brightest.
Being next to you
is a constant reminder
of God's greatest love and mercy.
How He listens to prayers,
and answers them in ways beyond measure.

# PART III – WHEN LOVE BECAME A MIRROR

It is days like this when I know
what loving hard really means.

Today, I feel my heart pounding with joy,
the excitement of loving another
as my feet hit the pavement
and I breathe in the warm, crisp air.

I smile thinking of my lover,
the one I choose to be in love with
without guilt or shame.

I am over the sky with happiness,
thrilled for all that is yet to come.

**Resting Place**

I will always find your soul
as my resting place,
where nothing else matters
but the time we spend.

I will find you in dark spaces,
hold tight to the love
we've shared over the years.

I will find you in the depths of sorrow,
and remember
that you smelled like heaven,
that the most beautiful places in the world
were copied from you.

I will remember how I loved you,
like your spirit was my own.
We shared the same broken heart,
stitched together
with fantasies and fairy tales.

We used to be sad,
expecting far too much
from one another.

We found love
in a world that did not love us.
Black love was our forte
our revolution,
our prayer.

We found happiness
in a nontraditional sense.
We found acceptance
before we found each other.

Our love did not rely on one another,

because we relied on ourselves
and if you ask me,
that's the best kind of love:
the kind that asks for nothing
but joy.

**Swarming Bees**

Memories of the past come like swarming bees,
invading my space,
threatening to sting
and leave behind the burn.

I cannot get the nostalgia out of my mind
back when my only concerns
were classes
and him.
He was my boo at the time.

Still, loving him
was sometimes one-sided.
He did not have much to offer.

Being with him meant sleeping on floors,
complaining about the price of everything,
yet still wanting luxury.
He took advantage
of the chances I gave him
to enjoy this world.

I showed him the mountains
at Garden of the Gods.
We ate good chicken wings
and loved on a city
that was new and unfamiliar.

We talked all night
because it had been so long.

Then we explored the vibrant city
of New Orleans.
Took a bus tour,
and I got to see him smile.
We walked down Bourbon Street
and laughed at the chaos,

the comical scenes
and the wild characters
that fills that beautiful city.

We lay together under a full moon,
and I poured my heart out to him
for the last time.

And now we are strangers
who do not talk,
and don't spend time
in the same rooms.

Just memories
swarming, stinging.

## To an Old Friend

I love you still.
I see you are sober now, doing well.

The moments we shared are irreplaceable.
The void you left is indescribable.

But I pray that even if we never speak again,
you'll know I considered you a true friend.

## These Days

Things have changed since I last talked to you.
The color of life is more vibrant.
I am finally letting go of things
that were never mine to control.
I let them fly away in the wind.

I think about you often still,
wondering if you are still my friend.
If I saw you at the grocery store,
would we stop and exchange words?

Are you loving her the same these days?
When you hug her, does my face pop up?

I have a few suitors who want to know me,
yet I'm scared to let someone in,
mostly because I love too hard these days.

I wonder if you have learned
how to manage the chaotic life you seemed to have.
I wonder if you and her are still a thing.

I think about how happy you seemed
whenever you came around,
how your energy lit up the rooms
and even the world outside.

I think of how you claimed us friends,
and I wonder if you ever thought differently.

But now I know,
you were
the beautiful flower along the path
that I had to stop and admire,
but could not take with me, because you
belong to green pastures.

You deserve a chance at life,
a chance to grow in the sun
and become even more beautiful.
But I hope you know,
you're already so beautiful as you are.

I hope she tells you that every day,
I hope she values you the way I did, secretly.
I hope she hugs you at every chance,
holds you when you are vulnerable,
and lets you be a man.

I hope she loves you so much
that she cries at the thought of losing you.
If she cannot do those things,
then she is not the one,
then she should not have been the choice you made.

I hope she reassures you with constant kisses,
knows that she has something rare,
something precious,
something good.

I hope she calms your nerves on bad days,
encourages you to reach new heights.
I hope she knows
she has a rare flower in her hands,
something to treasure,
something delicate and beautiful.

Because she touched it,
she better know how to care for it.
And even if our paths never cross again,
I will smile knowing you are thriving,
that you are seen,
that you are loved
in the way you were always meant to be

## Natural Hair Journey

From the painful process of perms and relaxers
to the challenges of loving our natural,
from the beginning of time with beads and barrettes
to box braids and silk presses,
I learned to love my hair.

4C never changed textures,
even after so many alterations.
I have always had coarse hair,
sometimes hiding under hats and wigs,
yet missing the feeling of my own scalp,
the connection to the souls of the ones who came before.

In every strand, I've felt a million hands,
hands that came before me, shaping, nurturing.
My soul is deeply rooted in my hair.

Getting my hair done is my therapy,
my black girl therapy.

Every braid out, twist out, or afro
from puff to promises of style,
I was never content with just one look.
Every month, something new,
something different done to my hair.

My hair is
history,
resistance,
beauty in natural form.

It is crown and culture,
soft and strong at the same time.
No matter how I wear it,
pressed, braided, twisted, or free,
it will always be mine.

Rooted.
Royal.
Naturally me.

Sweet daughter,

you will never forget
the first time a man mentions marriage.
He will say it casually,
as if it costs him nothing,
with intentions that may or may not be pure.

Know this.
Your happiness should never be indebted
to the hope
of a man making you his wife.

Not his modern-day woman.
Not just his cooker,
his cleaner,
his home to carry his seeds.

You are so much more
than the modern wife they describe.

You will be a nurturer.
A woman who may spend her days
pouring into others.
But most importantly,
you must remember to pour into yourself.

Because your happiness is sacred.

Do not waste your life
catering to everyone else
and losing your identity in the process.

You will yearn for the woman
you never allowed yourself to become,
and it aches differently
when you discover her
too late.

That kind of regret turns into anger.
And anger, if unchecked,
spills onto everyone around you.

I want to save you
from hurting yourself
by giving you this truth.

Be whole before you are chosen.
Be fulfilled before you are claimed.
And never shrink your becoming
for the comfort of someone else.

## Tell Them

When they ask what they did wrong,
tell them,

It was the lack of care they had for you.

The tears that grew into puddles on pillows,
soaked with regret and heartbreak.

Tell them it was the unanswered calls,
the long hours spent in their waiting rooms,
hoping they would show up,
hoping they would care.

Tell them it was how they treated you
like your body mattered more than your mind,
like you were good enough to lay with
but never good enough to love.

Tell them it was the way they used you,
how they smiled when you undressed,
but sighed when you spoke of the future,
your goals,
your desire to build something lasting
and how you wanted them to be part of it.

Tell them about the time you spent alone,
healing yourself,
caring for your own wounds
while letting them inside your womb.

Tell them you have known pain,
from a long line of men
who came and went,
finding satisfaction only in their own needs.

Tell them you felt abandoned your whole life,
thought a wedding could cure that ache,

believed a husband meant you were set for life,
until you learned that piece of paper
didn't mean a thing.

Tell them you had your own light,
and that is why they chose you
they wanted to take it,
while pretending to care
how you got it.

But be honest:
you let them hold you back.
You let them use you.
It was your naive heart
that could not believe the truth.

When they left you with nothing,
you finally saw it
the truth your loved ones had shown you.

Now you chase the ghosts of the past,
believing they are the only ones who can save you.
But you have learned

life is more than the physical world.

Now you see a life shared with Spirit,
with a God who loves you,
with ancestors who walk beside you
still getting to know them,
still healing.

Tell them it took you years to get here.
Tell them it took your whole life.
But now you see

the pieces that were left broken,
you picked them up,
and built yourself again.

Tell the world:
it was your own love you were missing all along.
Now you are complete.
Whole.
Happy.
At peace.

**Woman**

He tried to make me lose it.

Once I found it, I held on to it
knowing the power it held,
I kept it captive.

Can't be giving this free love out
like refills.

I am the woman
the nurturer,
the lover,
the epitome of soft and feminine,
the original form of the rib from a man,
God's greatest creation.

## Too Much for Most

I know that love is hard,
and I fall fast.

A sly, charming smile
leaves me weak in the knees.
A gentleman who can make me laugh
always catches my attention.

I need him to feel like a man,
to move through life with authority,
to talk with me about everything,
what is under the sun and beyond it.

I love when he chases me,
but plays hard to get.

I do not need a man
still questioning his worth.
I once wanted to save them,
but I am done saving,
because no one saved me.

No one ever made me feel secure.
I always pursued men
who struggled in life,
without proper father figures,
without ambition,
content to stay stuck in a circle.

I dream of big houses and mountain views,
trips to the ocean,
family gatherings,
business meetings and speaking events,
fans and admirers from all over the world.

I have dreamed of making a difference
since I was a little girl.

I have a lot of personality,
and often I think
it is too much for most.

## LOVE

Have you ever fallen in love?
Have you ever tried hard not to say
those three words,
for fear they do not feel the same?

Have you ever drafted poems
about how good they make you feel,
hoping to read them at your wedding one day?

Have you ever consulted the Most High
to love them correctly?

Have you ever felt the feeling deep in your bones,
in your spirit,
and can no longer deny
that you have fallen?

One day I woke up,
and the love songs sounded real.

Have you ever dreamed of possibilities?
It did not matter that they had flaws
you would take every part of their imperfections
and create an amazing piece of artwork out of it.

Have you ever trusted everything they said?
Hung on to every word and action,
let them lead you
to whatever they wanted with you?

Have you ever smiled at a text?
Cried at words?
Blushed at new beginnings?
Hid from love?

Have you ever believed yourself to be good enough?

Have you ever loved someone in a way
that it made you question
the realness of love before?

Have you ever said, "I never met anyone like you,"
and meant it?

Have you ever paused after every sweet thing said?
Have you ever taken a chance with it?

Ever pictured your life with them,
wanted to lay in their bed until the sun came up,
every single night?

Desired to wake up and do life together,
get the kids ready for school,
kiss them before they go to work,
and at the end of each night
talk about your days?

Have you ever found a lover and a best friend?
Have you ever been in love and wanted someone
so much that you would
wait for the day they would make you theirs?

## A Beautifully Dressed Woman

They will never understand the hype
of a beautifully dressed woman,

how she enters a room, poised,
heads turn, her presence creates influence.

Bright colors have always been her thing.
She dresses to the T – as sweet as iced tea,
just as glamorous as she can be.

**Who She Used to Be**

The pain was my friend at one point.
I held onto her.

She sat with me in the nighttime.
She was there when they counted me out.

She told me false tales
how she would always be there for me.
So, I found it comforting,
that at least she would be around
when it seemed nobody else wanted to be.

Then I met love one day
and she was memorable.

Everyone wanted to be around her,
everyone wanted to have her.

She came one day when I thought I had
someone just like her,
but she showed me there can no other than her.

She made me smile.
She did not hurt like pain did.
She was full of joy
and fulfilled promises.
She was light in all the dark corners
that pain had left me in.

But see, without pain,
I would not have known love —
would never have recognized her,
would never have known the difference.

Pain taught me that love was of God.
Love taught me that pain was not forever.

## Every Now and Then

My ancestors did not die
for me to choose defeat.

A million men did not march
for me to give up so easily.

My pain is sewn into my roots
follicles of hope and despair.

I may not feel hopeful all day,
but I can muster up a grin
every now and then.

**A Table for Me**

No longer fighting for a spot
at a table where smiles turned into frowns,
and the food was cold,
the people are unwelcoming.

Instead, I will go where I'm used to sitting alone,
enjoying my meal in silence,
only bringing those around me
who truly love me.

All the fighting and tears to keep you
when you were destined to go.
I will never regret caring for you,
I will never regret trying.

But now I know I need time alone,
to truly heal the demons trying to creep in.
I have got a battle to fight
that does not include anyone but myself.

And one day,
I will rise like sunlight through the clouds,
smile with the ease of knowing
my heart is finally home,
my soul at peace,
ready to embrace the love I was always meant to keep.

**Decisions**

If you want to be with her.
if you love her, adore her,
think she is a better fit for the man
you aim to be in the highest form of love,
then I truly hope it works out for you.

I have spent a year trying to love you,
sending you all my prayers and wishes,
hopes and dreams,
visions and ambitions.

Most of the time we communicated,
shared intimate conversations,
laughed deep from the roots of care.
Joy was natural,
Connection divine.
But I guess we ran out of time.

You went back to your old flame
The one who hurt you,
and who you hurt.
The toxic relationship you could not let go of.

Meanwhile, I
Stayed right where I was, yet I grew
past the need for another man to occupy
the parts of me I now keep to myself.

I would be lying if I said I knew who he was.
I would also be lying if I said
I did not think it was you.

But I have been here before,
never made it out the rain with them.
We make love so hard,
By trying to show up in spaces
where we later find we are trespassers.

I will miss you in the summertime,
long for you in the winter,
still care about you come fall,
keep you in my memories, maybe forever.

I guess I will always be the one that got away,
love too strong for someone to hold onto,
love too deep that it drowns those around me.

But I will keep trying,
hoping for a spot in the realm of true love.
Keep believing that it is still out there for me.
But I do not want to hope and wish,
I want to decide.

Decide that love is for me.
Decide that it will be for me.
Decide that by the end of 2023,
when my commitment to be single and abstinent ends,
I will find the one
who is right for me.

**Catching Flights Not Feelings**

Catching flights, not feelings.
Booking trips, not therapy sessions.

Yet I have still sat down with the Most High
and talked things through.

From struggle grew the way to calm and clarity.
I had faith in what my eyes could not see.

I loved like I had never hurt before.
I gave unconditional love
when I never got it back in return.

I became enemies with those I have hurt,
just praying they forgive me.

I struggled to believe I deserved the good things
when my intentions were never messed up
to begin with.

So, I will keep catching flights, not feelings,
until the right love finds me
the kind that feels like a destination
I do not have to leave to feel free.

**To You**

I hope you are doing good.
I hope you are finally getting ahead.

Hope you passed that test.
Hope you finally get to rest
from all those vacations.

Hope your dog is doing better in the cold.
I hope you are healing
from the deaths of your loved ones recently.

I hope you are picking your head up,
taking care of yourself,
walking with confidence.

I hope you are financially secure.
I hope you are happy.

I wonder if you have smiled today.
I wonder if you are safe.

I hope you have found your flow,
I always knew you would.

I am finally getting the rest I have needed
finally comfortable alone.

I do not seek your heart anymore.
I am adjusting to you being gone.

First time I ever experienced heartbreak
from loving a man at an early age
I never knew what would become of
shattered wants and needs.

I never knew that through the darkness
there was the light of hope.

I had no idea that God would wait for me
at the end of the valleys
that were dark and felt deadly
that He would direct my direction,
instruct the instructions given.

That one day,
it would make me a better woman.

Every tear I cried would nourish
my plant of life.

That one day, a man would love me,
in his actions and with his words.

That I would not have to worry about the future;
I would be too busy enjoying the present.

That every poem I wrote about love,
would manifest into something
I could write about forever.

That dreams become wishes,
wishes become hopes,
and hopes become reality.

When I was left alone
inside our shared home,
while he worked until early mornings,
my mind began forming,
wondering about a life
outside of what I had.

I felt guilty,
convinced it was not that bad.

We would walk down the aisle
that rainy day in Spring,
convinced we would have it all ahead of us,
convinced we would have everything.

I loved him with intention,
despite the abrupt ending.
Thinking of him in random thoughts.
I hope he knows
the well wishes I am sending.

I did not have healthy love to give back then,
unfamiliar with who I was,
I found myself constantly conforming.

The day I learned accountability,
I breathed again,
it felt reforming.

I was responsible
for the ultimate crash and burn.
I will take the blame,
because I have learned
that even good decisions
hold both joy and pain,
and God will always be my sunshine
after every seasonal rain.

# PART IV – WHERE THE POEMS GREW

**Daughter**

I just hope you spread your wings,
I just hope you do impactful things.

Lovely being,
I will love you always.
Never be afraid to love, baby girl;
It is a beautiful thing.

I learned to love another
by loving you.
Before you,
my heart sang the blues.

I cannot say enough how much I care for you,
I will show it.
You are the most beautiful girl in the world
I hope you know it.

Be great, my love.
Refuse to let this life bring you down.
I hope to be around for you,
when others try to pull you to the ground.

You are still so young now,
yet I can already see your light
in your heart,
and in your eyes.

There is nothing in this world you cannot do.
Test your luck on the impossible.
As long as you have a mind,
you are unstoppable.

So, live the life you want to live,
my daughter.

**A Gentle Man**

A gentle man
does not let you touch a single door.
He walks closer to the street,
pumps your gas,
and amazed by your style and grace.

He holds your hand,
calls you beautiful,
calls you back when he says he will.

He talks to you every night,
knowing that to get close to you,
he must first know who God is.

He does not rush you out of your clothes.
He adores his mama.
Understands the roles of a true family.

He takes care of the children he fathers.
He compliments your clothing
rather than criticize.

## Sunflowers & Black Women

Black women
we love sunflowers.
We always look good in yellow, simply because
we are beautiful and brown at the core,
and bright as the sun on the outside.

When we step outside,
the sun warms our skin from deep within.
Perspiration from the rain gives us strength.
We wish upon stars and moons,
tied to the soil our ancestors stepped on
rooted in the family trees of generations.

The mothers in my bloodline
loved on their daughters and sons,
teaching them they hold power,
that they are indeed the ones.

I come from a past of fighters and lovers,
souls shaped by hard work
and unshakable perseverance.

## Expired Grief

Is it right to think that grief expires?
That even though they cannot count the days on my calendar,
It does not mean the memory of you has retired.
I know time has passed since your transition,
Even your name is barely mentioned.
I will never forget your existence.
You are what is always missing.

## The Difference

In the past, it was easy to say
if he walked away, I would be a good girl and stay.

Beyond the expiration date,
way past the time it took to understand
how I was being treated was not okay.

God sent me a man who feels like home
a man I do not have to tell,
"I don't want to be alone."

A man who loved me
before he knew physically
what the inside of my body felt like.

A man who played the game so well,
I realized the cards had never been dealt right.

He knew belief was the only way to keep me
and I knew through God was the only way
to see me.

I lacked a spiritual connection every time,
thought because they made me laugh
they cared about my mind.

But there is a difference
between a man who claims to love God,
and a man who really gives God all his time.

I wanted to tell him I loved him for weeks now,
afraid it was too soon, so I kept it secret
praying it would not seep out.

He held me with purpose,
like I deserved it.

## Society's Standard

I am not society's prototype.
I am not the standard you have been made to believe.

I may share similarities,
but I am me.

Society is not my creator,
though I live within its systems.

Navigating my way through it
leads me to ultimate wisdom.

## Uncertainties

In a world full of uncertainties,
we found a life we wanted.

I found a home full of love and laughter,
and you found acceptance from the world.

And somewhere in between,
we found each other.

Although I know the truth of it all,
I'll pretend with you.
Pretend that what we have doesn't exist.
Pretend we are our best selves without each other.

And maybe that is true.

Maybe loving each other
was never about staying,
but about showing one another
what was possible.

So in this world of uncertainties,
I will let the truth sit softly beside me,
and I'll let the pretending
be gentle.

He came into my life one day,
and I stood taller.
I walked with more grace,
my mind sharpened.
I felt more like a woman.

I grew patience,
more understanding.

He is the only one I see.
The sun shines brighter,
the moon illuminates,
and the night stars pop out more.

I love
knowing he is near,
even in the quiet moments
when words are few.

He has helped me shape my life
into something brighter,
and I am forever grateful
for this King.

## Adora

Adora, have I told you that you are beautiful lately?
Have I told you the sky lights up when you wake,
That being your mother was fate.

Dora, have I told you that I prayed you were a girl,
I wanted to put little pink bows in your hair,
Dress you up so you are ready for the world.

Adora, have I told you that we knew you were special,
That each day you get prettier and smarter,
Your soul becomes gentler.

I sang "My Sunshine" to you in my womb,
How beautiful it is to have a spirit,
That plays a wonderful tune,
and has many phases like the moon.

Adora, you brought light into the darkness,
Softness where life tries to harden,
A beautiful view that is you,
A precious life that is anew.

**Forever**

What does sharing forever with someone really mean?

The days are long, the decisions made,
that through the many years of my life,
you will be a part of it.

We would never know goodbyes,
only see-you-laters.

If destiny finds us together, it is God-sent.
Never leave me or forsake me.

You are a man
that a woman once loved.

I cannot dream much about you,
You are here in the real world with me.

I once wanted love and lovemaking all in one,
like one big blanket comforting me,
snuggled up against your version of love.

**Flawed**

Would he love me and all my flaws?
My occasional depression,
and my recent health issues.

My earlier tries at marriage,
my child out of wedlock.

Would he love me in all of my flaws?
My flaws that make me human,
My flaws that have become a part of my story.

My flaws that may cause others to frown,
And some others to lean towards me.

Flaws mean I have lived my life.
Flaws that mean my blood is pumping.

My heart is full and hopeful.
My flaws are written in red ink,
left in previous chapters.
No need to return.
The real meaning is in the ending,
Where I can choose new beginnings.

## 333

Angel numbers in my dreams,
It seems,
My love for him flowed like streams.
He was everything to me,
I mean,
He was a huge part of my heart.

**Your Absence**

When you left,
you took the promise
of more days with you.

You carried my heart with you,
so needy and vulnerable,
Without you.

Wishes start to feel like insanity
when you know
you will never receive them,
not in this lifetime.

I just hope you knew
how much I loved you.
I hope I did what was right
in your absence.

Every connection you built
ended too soon,
and I'm left asking
why it always had to end.

Why can't Heaven take phone calls?
I would dial you just to say
I miss your infectious laugh.

Making you proud
has become my motivation.
Mourning you
has become my routine.

I would ask if you are okay.
If up there,
you can let go of the bad memories.
Because when you left,
all the small, negative things

became just that,
small.

I have not cried in a week.
Next week marks a year.

And still,
every minute of your absence
makes me reach
for one more second.

The day he starts giving excuses
for why he did not show up,
or call,
or text you back,

the day he makes being with him harder,
and you stop loving him in a way
that makes you smile,
that makes you happy to be by his side

That is the day you leave.

And you take all of you with you.

Not everyone is meant to stay forever.
Some are just fleeting moments in time.

So, enjoy them while they are there.
Love hard.
Care deeply.

Find true love in the ones
you hug,
spend time with,
and have important conversations with.

Those are the ones you will never forget.

**Happiest Birthday**

For my birthday, God gave me flowers
painted on steps off the highway:
bright pinks and blues,
yellows and browns,
all drawn perfectly.

He made sure my eyes could see,
while driving the back roads, listening to music.

For my birthday, God gave me a poem,
so beautiful I believed it was made just for me.
Despite the thousands of views,
I just knew.

For my birthday, God gave me encouragement.
Through the community around me,
I was shown that even through the storms,
I can take cover and wait for them to pass.

For my birthday,
the God of the universe gave me gifts
in the form of red cardinals,
gorgeous bluebirds,
and yellow butterflies.

For my birthday, God appreciated me
in every eye that looked my way,
every word of admiration spoken to me,
in the meals my friends cooked for me,
the time they took to listen.

The joy I felt that they trusted me,
that I was someone worthy
of the best birthday.

On my birthday, God gave me a full moon,
shining stars in the sky,

bright clouds I have always loved,
a life I have always wanted
but never knew I could have.

God gave me love on my birthday
in family and friends,
in their thoughtfulness and sweet actions.

**My Daddy's Recipes**

He was a light that cannot be replaced.
I must say,
he had a spirit that could not be dismayed.

My father who supported all my hopes and dreams,
he bought my first typewriter,
gifted me with my first sewing machine.

The first one to tell me, "Don't you cry over no boy!"
He was the one at track meets with fruit,
for the team to enjoy.

He was well known for his cooking skills,
Breakfast dishes, pies and
his talent on barbecue grills.

He would call and say, "I cooked for a neighbor today"
His heart was what I loved,
his love language shown on display during holidays.

My daddy made the best of everything,
and although,
we never got all his recipes,
he left us with a few things.

If we mix up all the ingredients that made up who he was,
we would understand just what a good recipe does.

It is good on the soul,
bringing joy to our hearts,
leaving an impact,
that will never depart.

That is who my daddy was to those he met,
a chef but yet,
a man who lived with no regrets.

Whether you liked his hamburgers, ribs,
or sauces galore,
Remember him as a man who loved to explore.

As he traveled the world and enjoyed cuisine,
or cooked in his kitchen or in Maxine's.

He was a lover of life and people too,
It is never goodbye,
but always,
sweet and good memories,
that will get us through.

# ABOUT THE AUTHOR

Brandy Harris is a poet and writer whose work explores themes of personal growth, emotional resilience, and the transformative power of love and faith. Her poetry is deeply reflective, offering insight into the human experience, including heartbreak, healing, and self-discovery.

As a mother, wife, and advocate for intentional living, Brandy draws on her own journey to bring forth the complexities of relationships, accountability, and personal transformation. Her writing invites readers to engage with their own stories, encouraging reflection, growth, and the pursuit of wholeness.

Through her work, Brandy emphasizes the power of vulnerability and the beauty that emerges when we confront our challenges with honesty and courage. Her poetry collection offers both an intimate and universal exploration of life's emotional landscape, bridging personal experience with broader human truths.

www.ingramcontent.com/pod-product-compliance
Lightning Source LLC
LaVergne TN
LVHW090532110826
845146LV00003B/1069

* 9 7 9 8 2 3 4 0 1 8 7 3 1 *